Photo by Romulus Linney
Scott Sowers and Adrienne Thompson in the Theater for the New City production of "Three Poets." Set design by Anne C. Patterson.

THREE POETS

THREE PLAYS
BY **ROMULUS LINNEY**

★

★

DRAMATISTS
PLAY SERVICE
INC.

THREE POETS
Copyright © 1990, Romulus Linney

All Rights Reserved

CAUTION: Professionals and amateurs are hereby warned that performance of any or all of the Plays in the volume THREE POETS is subject to payment of a royalty. The Plays are fully protected under the copyright laws of the United States of America, and of all countries covered by the International Copyright Union (including the Dominion of Canada and the rest of the British Commonwealth), and of all countries covered by the Pan-American Copyright Convention, the Universal Copyright Convention, the Berne Convention, and of all countries with which the United States has reciprocal copyright relations. All rights, including professional/amateur stage rights, motion picture, recitation, lecturing, public reading, radio broadcasting, television, video or sound recording, all other forms of mechanical or electronic reproduction, such as CD-ROM, CD-I, DVD, information storage and retrieval systems and photocopying, and the rights of translation into foreign languages, are strictly reserved. Particular emphasis is placed upon the matter of readings, permission for which must be secured from the Author's agent in writing.

The English language stock and amateur stage performance rights in the United States, its territories, possessions and Canada for the Plays in the volume THREE POETS are controlled exclusively by DRAMATISTS PLAY SERVICE, INC., 440 Park Avenue South, New York, NY 10016. No professional or nonprofessional performance of any or all of the Plays may be given without obtaining in advance the written permission of DRAMATISTS PLAY SERVICE, INC., and paying the requisite fee.

Inquiries concerning all other rights should be addressed to The Gersh Agency, 41 Madison Avenue, 33rd Floor, New York, NY 10010. Attn: Peter Hagan.

SPECIAL NOTE
Anyone receiving permission to produce any or all of the Plays in the volume THREE POETS is required to give credit to the Author as sole and exclusive Author of the Play(s) on the title page of all programs distributed in connection with performances of the Play(s) and in all instances in which the title(s) of the Play(s) appears for purposes of advertising, publicizing or otherwise exploiting the Play(s) and/or a production thereof. The name of the Author must appear on a separate line, in which no other name appears, immediately beneath the title(s) and in size of type equal to 50% of the size of the largest, most prominent letter used for the title(s) of the Play(s). No person, firm or entity may receive credit larger or more prominent than that accorded the Author.

THREE POETS was first produced at the Theater for the New City (Crystal Field and George Bartenieff, Artistic Directors) in New York City in November, 1989. It was directed by Romulus Linney; the set and costume designs were by Anne C. Patterson; the lighting design was by David Finley; and the production stage manager was Ellen Melaver. The casts were as follows:

KOMACHI
KOMACHI .... Adrienne Thompson
KOMACHI'S VOICE .... Kathleen Chalfant
SHOSHO .... Scott Sowers

HROSVITHA
GERBERGA .... Kathleen Chalfant
HROSVITHA .... Mary Fosket
BROTHER WILLIAM .... John MacKay
ABRAHAM .... Scott Sowers
MARY .... Adrienne Thompson

AKHMATOVA
PECDOV .... John MacKay
MARYA .... Adrienne Thompson
RUDINSKY .... Scott Sowers
KLARINA .... Mary Fosket
ANNA AKHMATOVA .... Kathleen Chalfant

SCENE DESIGN

KOMACHI is written for a Japanese Noh mask. If the mask cannot be spoken through, the character of Komachi may be divided: one actress on stage, wearing the mask, another to one side speaking her lines. The play may also be done with Komachi wearing a much different kind of mask, with both characters masked or without masks at all.

The carpet in HROSVITHA should be thick and soft, since much of the action takes place upon it.

The furniture of the Commissar's inquisition room in AKHMATOVA should be very elegant, at odds with its purpose.

The staging of these plays can take any number of forms. None should be scenically overburdened. The world they create should be poetic in the best sense: elemental, eloquent and simple.

The plays should be performed without intermission.

KOMACHI

from the Komachi Noh plays of Japan

for Scott Sowers

CHARACTERS

KOMACHI
SHOSHO

AUTHOR'S NOTE: If the masked KOMACHI cannot speak clearly, a third character, in black, is KOMACHI'S VOICE.

PLACE

A seashore in Japan.

TIME

9th Century.

KOMACHI

Sound of waves and sea birds.

A seashore tree stump. Below it, three seaworn rocks, and lying across them, a medieval Japanese sword in its scabbard.

Darkness. Silence. A flute plays.

Light appears, very slowly, on Komachi, who is wearing a Noh mask of a beautiful young woman. She wears a black kimono and has a white scarf around her waist.

Beside her stands Prince Shosho. He is not masked. He has a red scarf over one shoulder. He now has the sword and scabbard in his belt.

Flute stops.

      KOMACHI
     In the spring
 young men come running
       to love
      and kill
    young women.

       SHOSHO
     In the spring
  young women wait
    like spiders
 to trap young men.

KOMACHI
Only the poet
who writes about love
when young —

SHOSHO
can write about life
when old.

KOMACHI
It takes one
to understand the other.

(The flute plays again. Komachi moves downstage and sits on the tree stump. Shosho follows, and formally addresses her.)

SHOSHO
I have come
beautiful Komachi
to pay my respects.
Shosho
Third Son of the Emperor
Prince of this kingdom.

(Komachi nods.)

KOMACHI
It is good of you
to visit me.

SHOSHO
Komachi!
You are the greatest beauty
in Japan!
One of the Six Poetic Geniuses
of our age.
I love you!
I will have you
and no one else!

KOMACHI
Prince, be careful.
When you know me
You might not want me.

SHOSHO
In love with you
I too am a poet!
You have inspired me!
I have written this!!

(Shosho kneels and declaims passionately.)

I see you in my sleep!
I hold you in my arms!
Let me love you now
Like I do in my dreams!

(Shosho looks at Komachi. She shakes her head slightly.)

KOMACHI
I slept, in love with you,
and oh, you appeared before me.
Had I known
it was a dream
Nothing could have waked me.

(Shosho nods.)

SHOSHO
That is better.

KOMACHI
Yes it is.

(Shosho declaims again, even more passionately.)

SHOSHO
I am on fire!
My body burns for you
And you won't have me!
I am filled with pain
All this moonlit night!

(He looks at her. Komachi shakes her head.)

KOMACHI
Through these dark nights
I sleep and wake
my passion rising
face on fire
a heart charred wood
turning black.

(Shosho sits up, nods.)

SHOSHO
That too is better.

KOMACHI
Yes it is.

SHOSHO
Very well!
Since you know
so much about love
tell me what it is,
in one poem!

KOMACHI
Very well.
He forgot about me.
And I was so sure he wouldn't.
Now all I do is wonder
if I exist.

SHOSHO
That is a poem?

KOMACHI
Yes it is.

SHOSHO
You think *that* is love?

KOMACHI
Yes I do.

SHOSHO
No! Love is a storm, a thunderbolt!
It strikes and crushes!
You are trying to make my desire foolish.
My passion ridiculous.

KOMACHI
Your passion is military not amatory.
Lovers without poetry
are trouble enough.
With it
they are exhausting.

SHOSHO
You take this disdainful attitude
toward those who love you?

KOMACHI
Yes I do.

SHOSHO
And write poem after poem about love
yourself?

KOMACHI
Yes I will.

SHOSHO
And you alone
know what love is?

KOMACHI
I alone
know that I alone
will love freely,
and not be conquered
by anyone's passion,
no matter how deeply felt
they think it may be.

SHOSHO
This only means
you love someone else.
The man who forgot about you.
What about him?

KOMACHI
Oh.
Outside it stays the same
inside it crumbles away
that is the flower
of a man's heart
in this world.

SHOSHO
Then forget him!
Forget every man you have ever met
but me!
I would die for you!

KOMACHI
No one
dies for love.
Some live for it,
falling in love

over and over and over,
as I do,
happy only then
but we die of other causes.

SHOSHO
How can you
make fun of me,
of this fire blazing
inside me!

KOMACHI
You want something you can't have.
and it burns.
You call it fire,
but I think
it has more to do
with impatience
than with passion.

SHOSHO
And you will write poems
insulting me.

KOMACHI
Yes, I will.

(Pause.)

Give in? Lie down?
like a ripple on a lake
to a passing wind?
There are no fish in these waters.
I'm not here either.
Can't you see that?
Coming here
on your fisherman feet.

SHOSHO
You will refuse me,
a Prince of this Kingdom?

KOMACHI
Yes I will.

SHOSHO
I can take you by force!

KOMACHI
And disgrace yourself forever?
In this life and the one to come?

SHOSHO
But in the life to come
those who perished
enraged with passion
must linger
between life and death,
to wear out their humiliation
and take their revenge.

(Komachi moves away from Shosho.)

KOMACHI
Horrible man!

(Change of light: the stage is streaked with sharp-edged slants of light and shadow. Sound of waves. Komachi goes to the seashore rocks, standing on the other side of them from Shosho.)

I will run from you,
to a house in a forest,
on an island
in the sea.

SHOSHO
And I will follow you!

(He follows her.)

KOMACHI
Here, across the waves
I turn and watch
To see if you will really come.

SHOSHO
There is no bridge.
How will I find you?

(He looks at the rocks.)

The rocks! I will pick them up one by one
and one by one with bloody hands
build a bridge to your door.
Up! Down! Bend! Work!

(He moves the rocks about.)

Tearing the land from itself
until the earth itself reaches out
as my pathway to your bed.

(He stops, looks at her.)

The bridge is finished.
Now you know I will find you.

KOMACHI
Now I know you will find me!

SHOSHO
Is the moon down?
Yes, darkness!

KOMACHI
Now you can come to me.
In the moonlight you can lead
your horse through the shadows.

(Shosho puts the red scarf around his neck.)

SHOSHO
Look how I go to you!
My scarf at my throat!

KOMACHI
Black wind, rising waves,
They will not keep you from me.

SHOSHO
On I journey
across my bridge
to your island forests
through showers of leaves.
Leading my horse
I see you watching from your window —

KOMACHI
As the storm breaks!

(Shosho struggles against an imaginary storm.)

SHOSHO
Waves pound the shore!
The wind rises —

KOMACHI
Blowing your scarf
out behind your throat —

SHOSHO
Lightning flashes!
I see you
beautiful and scornful!
Mocking me!

KOMACHI
The wind! The waves!

SHOSHO
The storm!

KOMACHI
The rocks are wet and slippery!

SHOSHO
My horse is frightened!

KOMACHI
He rears up!

SHOSHO
His hooves thrash in the air!

KOMACHI
His hooves strike your face!

(Shosho falls to his knees. He screams. Then he holds out the red scarf.)

SHOSHO
And my scarf is red with blood.

(Shosho tosses the scarf on the rocks. He sits back and looks at it. Komachi goes to Shosho. She kneels beside him. Together they look at the scarf. Sound of waves.)

KOMACHI
Your head was torn
from your body.

SHOSHO
My blood washed away
in the waves.

(They sit, staring at the scarf. Lights up. Waves stop. They look at each other.)

KOMACHI
How was I guilty
of your ridiculous death?

SHOSHO
You laughed at me.
But could you forget me?

KOMACHI
No.

SHOSHO
You live!

KOMACHI
I live!

SHOSHO
Badly!

KOMACHI
Badly!

SHOSHO
Write a poem about that!

(Komachi holds out the white cloth. The flute plays again.)

KOMACHI
Alone and miserable
I cut my roots away,
and float like a reed on a stream.
When water asks me
I follow it anywhere.

(She puts the white cloth over her head, and bends over, an old woman.)

SHOSHO
You become famous
You live for a hundred years.

KOMACHI
Like a beggar.
My black hair turns white.
Skin coarse, face wrinkled.

SHOSHO
At a Festival
you watch a child dance.
Those watching you
are enlightened.
You are still beautiful,
but do not think so.

KOMACHI
Aching and stinking
I am filthy among outcasts
who look at me with disgust.

(Komachi bends over, walks about.)

SHOSHO
In the great cities you hide yourself
afraid someone will see you.
"Look! There she is!
Beautiful Komachi!"

KOMACHI
No! No!
Age and guilt want silence,
and no one to ask
who I am
traveller so wretched.

SHOSHO
Because you destroyed
the man who loved you!

KOMACHI
But I did not!
I did nothing to you!

SHOSHO
You laughed at me!!

(Komachi journeys, painfully.)

Walking, walking, behind the trees,
past lovers tombs and autumn hills —

KOMACHI
Above rivers flowing beside you
like this one —

SHOSHO
You see the boats rise and fall
on the currents
in the moonlight.

(Komachi stops at the rocks, leans forward. She bends over further, seeing something in the water.)

What's that?

KOMACHI
There, in the water!

SHOSHO
What's floating toward you there?

KOMACHI
It crawls down the yellow river
like a snake in a stream!

SHOSHO
Like a scarf!

(Shosho stands up. Komachi stares, kneeling.)

KOMACHI
A red scarf!

SHOSHO
And you see —

KOMACHI
I see
floating on a scarf of blood,
your head and mine.

(Shosho draws his sword and scabbard from his belt.)

SHOSHO
Legends of Komachi say
your head was struck from your body
by a bandit robbing graves.

KOMACHI
He was in fact
a Prince returned to earth
for that moment.

(Shosho holds up his sword.)

SHOSHO
Above you I stand,
your death in my arms.

(He lays the sword in its scabbard on her shoulder.)

KOMACHI
An icy fist
hits my neck
and I am gone!

SHOSHO
Your hair I cut off for pillows.
Your skull I throw to the river.

KOMACHI
Where it washes out into the sea
and then to a rocky beach
and there it stays
forever.

(Sound of waves.)

SHOSHO
And through your eyes
the tall grasses grow.

KOMACHI
So when the wind sweeps in
from the sea —

SHOSHO
They move and bend in your skull —

KOMACHI
And oh, how that hurts!

SHOSHO
Now with a bandit sword
in the shock of an instant
I deliver you from earth to eternity
and to me.

KOMACHI
Only the poet
who writes about love
when young.

SHOSHO
Can write about life
when old.

KOMACHI
It takes one
to understand the other.

The flute plays again. Komachi rises and takes the red scarf to the seashore stump. Shosho follows her, sword in hand.

Both turn their backs. Komachi takes off her mask and sets it on the red scarf, staring upward. Shosho now draws the blade of his sword from its scabbard and holds it up. It flashes in the light.

A heavy burst of drums and Japanese music.

Komachi and Shosho move quickly into darkness, leaving one shaft of light falling on the mask of the poet, staring at eternity.

HROSVITHA

from her play ABRAHAM

for Adrienne Thompson

CHARACTERS

GERBERGA, Abbess of Gandersheim
HROSVITHA, a nun
BROTHER WILLIAM, a monk
ABRAHAM, a hermit
MARY, his niece

PLACE
The free convent of Gandersheim, in Saxony.

TIME
Toward the end of the 10th century.

HROSVITHA

Shadows. Nuns sing Ave Maria Stella, *a Benedictine chant, or some other medieval chant, perhaps without words, sung by one woman. It is quiet and beautiful.*

A thick carpet is unfolded, and set down. On each side of the carpet, facing each other, are set two wooden Gothic chairs.

Light falls on the rug, shafts of light on the two chairs. Above them, a stained glass rose window appears.

Enter Gerberga, Abbess of Gandersheim. She is a regal figure, in a white medieval cowl, with a surplice of scarlet over her black robes. With her is Brother William, a monk in a plain robe, whose hood hides his face.

Gerberga walks with Brother William to one of the chairs and indicates that he may sit there. Then she moves, slowly, formally, to the other chair. They both sit.

The Nuns stop singing.

GERBERGA. Most dearly beloved Brother William. Of all the nuns in this convent, our Sister Hrosvitha is the only one whose behavior any Bishop might consider questionable. She is a writer. She composes devotional poems, all of them above reproach. But she is also writing a play, based on pagan Roman models, and I can see how your Bishop, since he has heard of it, may be alarmed. Let us see if there is anything to be alarmed about. Will you hear our Sister describe her work? *(Brother William nods.)* Sister. *(Enter Hrosvitha. She is composed but she is thrilled by this event. She stands above the rug, at its center, and speaks to Brother William.)*

HROSVITHA. My play is called Abraham. It is written to be performed by the Sisters of the Convent, with music composed for it here. I will gladly tell you its story. It is very beautiful, since I wrote it for God and his glory, and I know that you will like it. *(She smiles, excited by her tale.)* Abraham is a hermit. He has a niece called Mary. *(Around her, the lights change. They bathe her in a warm storytale glow, and light the rug brightly.)* When she is a child, Mary's parents die. Abraham adopts her. He builds a little cell for her, near his own, where he watches over her, hears her prayers and instructs her in divine law. *(Enter Mary, dressed in white and seen only by Hrosvitha. She kneels.)* Under his care, Mary becomes beautiful and devout. Abraham hears her prayers and her hymns every day, and thanks God for the happiness she gives him, for he wants her to enter a convent and become the bride of Christ. *(Enter Abraham, in a hermit's robe, holding a cross. Over his back hang a cloak and a large-brimmed hat. He also is only seen by Hrosvitha. He kneels.)* "I am happy," says Mary. "My Guardian Abraham means —"
MARY.   — means everything to me. I love to worship and study and pray and be near him.
HROSVITHA.   "I am happy," says Abraham. "My niece Mary means —"
ABRAHAM.   — everything to me. I love to worship and study and pray and be near her.
MARY.   I will always do whatever he says.
ABRAHAM.   I will send her to God, in heaven. *(Mary turns her back.)*
HROSVITHA.   One day, when Mary is seventeen years old, Abraham has a vision. *(Abraham moves in front of Hrosvitha, throws his arm in front of his eyes and kneels.)*
ABRAHAM.   Ah! *(Hrosvitha stands behind him, seeing his vision with him.)*
HROSVITHA.   A huge, dragon-like monster, with a horrifying stench —
ABRAHAM.   — rushes violently toward me! He wants to eat a little dove I have tied to my wrist. *(He acts it out.)* He knocks me over, seizes my little bird in his jaws and devours it!
HROSVITHA.   Then he vanishes, in smoke!

ABRAHAM. When I open my eyes, I am blind. I throw myself into prayer, for two days. Then, exhausted, I fall asleep. *(He does.)*
HROSVITHA. And he dreams he sees the beast again. But now, it is lying at his feet, no longer terrible or frightening. Just a huge, sleeping animal.
ABRAHAM. And the dove is flying to heaven, safe and free! I awake, weeping, and I can see again!
HROSVITHA. He wonders what the vision means!
ABRAHAM. Oh, the most awful uneasiness takes hold of me. Thinking of the monster asleep, and the dove free, I remember Mary, my little niece, my pupil. For three days, I haven't heard her praying or singing.
HROSVITHA. He goes to her cell! He knocks at her window! *(Abraham moves to an imaginary cell.)*
ABRAHAM. Mary? My child? Mary? Why won't you answer me? Mary?
HROSVITHA. She's gone!
ABRAHAM. Mary! *(He paces back and forth in anguish.)* What wolf has stolen my Mary? What devil has defiled her?
HROSVITHA. A hypocrite!
ABRAHAM. In a monk's robe?
HROSVITHA. He came to her with prayers and sugared words! He made the girl fall in love with him!
ABRAHAM. Mary, in love?
HROSVITHA. He seduced her and he abandoned her! When Mary realized what she had done, she tore her hair, dug her nails into her face and ran away!
ABRAHAM. Oh, Mary!
HROSVITHA. She is gone, Abraham.
ABRAHAM. Where?
HROSVITHA. Into the world. She has fallen.
ABRAHAM. Fallen? How?
HROSVITHA. It hurts me to tell you this.
ABRAHAM. Please!
HROSVITHA. She lives in an inn, where she sells herself to strange men.
ABRAHAM. Strange men? My Mary?

HROSVITHA. It comes naturally to whores. There is nothing you can do.
ABRAHAM. There is! I can go to that place!
HROSVITHA. They won't let you in!
ABRAHAM. If I pay them, they will! As a *lover* they will let me in!
HROSVITHA. That will break your vows! *(He hands her his cross.)*
ABRAHAM. Then I will break my vows! *(Abraham holds up a wide-brimmed hat that has been hanging from his shoulders, and spreads his cloak around his hermit's robe.)* With my face hidden by this hat, and my robe by this cloak, I will go to that place and bring her back to me, and to God! *(He turns away.)*
HROSVITHA. Mary! Come at once. You have a visitor. *(Mary turns around. She sweeps a colorful and sensuous shawl over her white dress. She moves down to the carpet. Abraham turns and comes onto the carpet. Hrosvitha, holding the cross, stands above and between them.)*
MARY. You wanted me?
ABRAHAM. That's right. I've paid for you and for some women to sing for us. What's your name?
MARY. Mary.
ABRAHAM. Give me your hand, Mary.
MARY. Take off the hat, Mister.
ABRAHAM. Later.
MARY. You can keep it on in bed for all I care. *(Mary meets Abraham at the center of the carpet, and takes his hand.)*
ABRAHAM. Mary!
MARY. Oh! *(Holding hands, they turn from each other.)*
ABRAHAM. My Mary!
HROSVITHA. His hand is strong!
MARY. What's happening to me?
HROSVITHA. He feels like silk!
ABRAHAM and MARY. Ah!
HROSVITHA. They remember happiness.
ABRAHAM. *(To himself.)* Talk to her! Say something!
HROSVITHA. He tries to play the lecher!
ABRAHAM. So, what are we waiting for?

HROSVITHA. She the whore!
MARY. Nothing! *(She turns away and weeps.)*
ABRAHAM. Now what's the matter? I want to go to bed with you, not watch you cry!
MARY. I'm all right now. A little thing moved me, very silly. Come on, my friend. Let's go.
ABRAHAM. Where's the bedroom?
MARY. This way, Mister. *(Leading Abraham by the hand, Mary takes him in a circle.)*
HROSVITHA. She takes him by the hand! They pass through a dark hallway, climb some stairs, and enter her bedroom! *(Mary leads Abraham to the center of the rug.)*
MARY. So lie down.
ABRAHAM. All right. *(He lies down on the carpet.)*
HROSVITHA. Music! *(The slow and beautiful chant is heard again.)*
MARY. Is that the music you want to hear?
ABRAHAM. Yes.
MARY. While we make love, Mister?
ABRAHAM. Yes.
MARY. No accounting for tastes. Well, you ready?
ABRAHAM. Yes. *(Mary moves toward him, smiling.)*
MARY. Now I get to take off that hat! *(Mary takes off his hat, and kisses him, eyes closed. Abraham does not move. Mary opens her eyes. She sees the face she is kissing.)* Oh!
ABRAHAM. Mary! It's me! I'm here! *(Mary throws herself down, away from him, head in her arms.)*
MARY. Oh! Oh!
ABRAHAM. Don't you know me?
MARY. God!
ABRAHAM. The man who loved you! Who wanted to marry you to the King of Heaven!
MARY. Leave me alone!
ABRAHAM. I *bought* you, remember? You're mine!
MARY. Ah! *(Mary curls up on the carpet, knees drawn up, arms over her head, crying.)*
ABRAHAM. Who was he?
MARY. Oh!

ABRAHAM. Who did this to you? A devil?
MARY. No, a man!
ABRAHAM. Why couldn't you trust me?
MARY. Oh!
ABRAHAM. If you'd told me, I would have prayed for you! I would have done penance for you!
MARY. Oh, stop!
ABRAHAM. No one but Christ lived without sin! We all sin! We fall! But we can repent, and rise again! Mary?
MARY. Go away!
ABRAHAM. I love you!
MARY. NO!!
ABRAHAM. What else but love could make me leave my cell, and break my vows? What else but love could make me, a hermit of God, come to this dreadful place and act like a lascivious fool? Mary, look at me!
MARY. I can't!
ABRAHAM. Come back to me! Ask God for his mercy! Or I will take your sins upon me! Anything! I've been a dead man without you!! *(The Nuns stop singing. Mary raises her head, and looks at Abraham.)*
MARY. I can't say no to you. I can't disobey you, or hurt you. *(She goes to his embrace, her head on his chest.)*
ABRAHAM. Mary!
MARY. I will come back to you! I want to! *(Abraham holds her in his arms.)*
ABRAHAM. I can see the window of your cell. That blessed place, where I come to see you every day. You smile at me and listen to me.
MARY. I pray and sing!
HROSVITHA. She will do it all again! *(Abraham stands, picks up his hat. Mary casts off her shawl.)*
ABRAHAM. I will take you to a convent, to be the bride of Christ.
MARY. Yes! I want to go there! Take me! *(Hrosvitha steps between them, with the cross.)*
HROSVITHA. Praise to the Son of God, and to His Mother the Queen of Heaven, who will never abandon those they love! Amen!

ABRAHAM and MARY. Amen! *(Abraham takes the cross. Exit Abraham and Mary. The lights change again, back to what they were when Hrosvitha began her story.)*
HROSVITHA. That is the end of my play. There will be music and the Sisters playing the parts will leave the stage.
GERBERGA. So. Brother William? *(No response. Gerberga gets up, walks about, thinking.)* I will admit, it's not quite clear. A sinner, Mary, is returned to God. But how? Under the persuasion of a holy man, who is a father to her, but who certainly does, like any other man, seduce her. This could suggest that women are seduced not only into sin and degradation but into sanctity and convents. And not just by holy men either, but by God, the greatest of Fathers. By Jesus, our perfect bridegroom, to whom we entrust our souls. I can see how a Bishop would be upset. *(Gerberga looks at Brother William. No response. Gerberga goes and sits in her chair again.)* Brother William? *(No response.)* Brother William? Are you asleep, sir?
BROTHER WILLIAM. I am *not* asleep! *(Brother William throws back his cowl, revealing his face.)* I have looked and I have listened. And I too am upset, but not about the play.
HROSVITHA. I am so relieved. My little play only echoes God's great love!
BROTHER WILLIAM. Your little play is hysterical female nonsense! No one in their right mind could care about anything so ridiculous!
HROSVITHA. Oh!
BROTHER WILLIAM. But what isn't ridiculous, and what I have waited patiently to talk about, Gerberga of Gandersheim, is that music!
GERBERGA. Music?
HROSVITHA. *Ave Maria Stella?*
BROTHER WILLIAM. A hymn to the Virgin, composed by you, which you will sing not only here, but outside your convent walls, in public worship!
GERBERGA. Brother William —
BROTHER WILLIAM. Your Bishop knows what you are doing.
GERBERGA. Brother William, do not speak to me like this.

BROTHER WILLIAM. He doesn't like it!
GERBERGA. Brother William, I beg you.
BROTHER WILLIAM. Secure in your wealthy convent of Canoness Nuns, you think you are a law unto yourselves! Your Bishop is deeply offended, and by you!
GERBERGA. And I, by him. Gandersheim is a free Abbey, given me by my King and my Pope. Who do you think you are talking to?
BROTHER WILLIAM. To a fool!
GERBERGA. Why am I a fool?
BROTHER WILLIAM. That music!
GERBERGA. What *about* that music?
BROTHER WILLIAM. It is blasphemous!
HROSVITHA. Oh!
GERBERGA. It is *what?*
BROTHER WILLIAM. You compose your own chants. You play them on the harp, the psalterium and the trumpet! Women, tooting trumpets to the glory of God? It is obscene and it is grotesque! In the words of the blessed Saint Paul: "Let the women keep silence in Church!"
GERBERGA. And why should we keep silent? Because we sing better here, write better here, LIVE better here, than you morose ugly men, with your dismal chants and your eternal hankering for domination and revenge? *(Brother William gets up.)*
BROTHER WILLIAM. You insolent and insubordinate nun! You will write no more Ave Marias!
GERBERGA. *(Gets up.)* I will go to the King!
BROTHER WILLIAM. And he will strip you of your authority!
GERBERGA. I will write to the Pope!
HROSVITHA. Please, stop!
BROTHER WILLIAM. And he will empty all of Gandersheim! Music in Church is for MEN and BOYS, as God's Holy Scripture plainly decrees! WOMEN! WE sing the chants! It is OUR voices and not YOURS that will be heard in the vaults of heaven! WOMEN!! BE SILENT!! *(Exit Brother William.)*
GERBERGA. A mad monk. Really. *(Hrosvitha falls to her knees, weeping.)*

HROSVITHA. What have I done?
GERBERGA. Nothing.
HROSVITHA. But the Bishop?
GERBERGA. If we followed every decree of every Bishop, we would live like soldiers, not like sisters. Depend on me. I will not abandon you. Continue your work! *(Hrosvitha kisses the hem of Gerberga's robe.)* As for this play, well. It can't be performed now. We will bind it, and put it in the Library. If the future should wonder what we did here, it will find your plays here. You are surely the first Sister, and perhaps the first woman, ever to write a play. And I am the arrogant Nun who preserved it. Yes, I like that idea very much. *(Pause. Gerberga starts out.)* Of course, I do have a few criticisms. Some of that language is very harsh. Smooth it out. And Abraham can't say out loud that he wants a woman. Change that. He just goes to get her, that's all. And that kissing. Do something about all that kissing! Ugh! *(Exit Gerberga.)*
HROSVITHA. Oh! *(She sits on the carpet, in frustration.)* OH!! *(She weeps. Lights change. Enter Abraham and Mary. They stand awkwardly watching her, looking at each other.)* OHHHHH! *(They sit with her on the carpet.)*
ABRAHAM. What's the matter?
MARY. Why are you crying?
HROSVITHA. Oh, be quiet!
MARY. She doesn't like us anymore.
ABRAHAM. Praise to the Son of God and the Queen of Heaven, who never abandon those they love.
MARY. Goodbye, stupid Abraham.
ABRAHAM. Goodbye, crazy Mary.
ABRAHAM and MARY. Not very nice!
HROSVITHA. Of course I love you! I danced and sang when you came to life! You know that!
ABRAHAM. Then what's wrong! *(Pause.)*
HROSVITHA. That horrible monk called you nonsense. My mother in Christ says you mustn't kiss. They don't know who you are! And neither do I!
ABRAHAM. We are yours.
MARY. Just as you are God's. He made you. You made us.

HROSVITHA. Badly.
MARY. Why?
HROSVITHA. *(Thinking it out.)* I don't know. I tried to write about love —
MARY. How love brings us to God!
HROSVITHA. What did you say?
ABRAHAM and MARY. How love brings us to God.
HROSVITHA. Maybe that's what's wrong. God is not always so simple, and love is not always so — beautiful. Go back!
ABRAHAM. Where?
HROSVITHA. I don't know! Father in Heaven! Help me! Abraham! A huge, dragon-like monster! *(Mary moves aside, kneels and prays. Abraham and Hrosvitha take up their positions at that moment in her play.)*
ABRAHAM. — rushes violently toward me! He wants to eat a little dove I have tied to my wrist. He knocks me over, seizes my little bird in his jaws, and devours it!
HROSVITHA. Then he vanishes, in smoke!
ABRAHAM. When I open my eyes, I am blind. I throw myself into prayer, for two days. Then, exhausted, I fall asleep.
HROSVITHA. And you dream you see the Beast again. But now — *(Hrosvitha stares at Abraham.)* just a huge, sleeping animal.
ABRAHAM. And the dove is flying to heaven, safe and free. *(Hrosvitha steps back. Abraham goes to Mary.)* Mary? *(Mary is praying.)* Mary!
MARY. Ah, Father Abraham! I am praying.
ABRAHAM. You may interrupt your prayers. Come with me.
MARY. Where are we going?
ABRAHAM. On a journey?
MARY. Where?
ABRAHAM. To another country. *(He puts on his hat and cloak, which disguise him.)*
MARY. Why are you doing that?
ABRAHAM. So no one will see who I am.
MARY. But why?
ABRAHAM. Hush. Trust in me. *(He takes her by the hand and they go into the brothel. He seats her on the carpet, and leaves her.*

Hrosvitha continues to rediscover her story.)
HROSVITHA. *He* takes her to the brothel! He pays a great deal of money to keep her there, for him! *(Mary puts on again the colorful harlot's shawl. Abraham moves away.)* She lives in the brothel. At first she still prays, but then she just waits, for his visits. *(Abraham goes to Mary.)* She is always glad to see him. *(Abraham creeps up behind her, puts his hand on over her eyes.)*
MARY.   Father Abraham!
ABRAHAM.   My darling Mary!
MARY.   It has been such a long time!
ABRAHAM.   Have you missed me?
MARY.   You know I have!
ABRAHAM.   Mary!
HROSVITHA.   Whorehouse! Music! Kiss! *(The Nuns sing once more. Abraham and Mary throw themselves into each other's arms, embrace wildly, and fall down on the carpet, kissing avidly.)*
ABRAHAM and MARY.   Ah! Ah! *(With his cloak lying over them, crying out in sexual pleasure, they make vigorous love.)*
HROSVITHA.   Better! *(There is a great deal of graphic pumping and heaving under the cloak, completed by a satisfying mutual orgasm, loudly proclaimed.)* The Beast devours the Dove!
ABRAHAM and MARY.   Ahhh! *(Abraham and Mary uncouple, and fall heavily away from each other, gasping until they get their breath. Then they look back at each other in amazement and fall back into each other's arms.)*
ABRAHAM.   Oh, God!
MARY.   How wonderful!
ABRAHAM.   I love you!
MARY.   I love you! *(Mary and Abraham lie exhausted together, in passionate contentment.)*
HROSVITHA.   And lies there, a huge sleeping animal.
ABRAHAM.   *(Groaning.)* Ahhh.
MARY.   *(Groaning.)* Ohhhhh.
HROSVITHA.   While the dove, safe and free, flies to heaven.
MARY.   Ahhhh!
ABRAHAM.   Ohhhh! *(Pause. The Nuns stop singing.)* Mary?
MARY.   Yes, my darling?
ABRAHAM.   I was a dead man without you.

MARY. *(Smiling.)* I remember.
ABRAHAM. I did not know what love was.
MARY. Neither did I.
ABRAHAM. It is the most wonderful thing in the world. *(Pause.)* But — *(He sighs.)*
MARY. But what?
ABRAHAM. I may not be coming here again.
MARY. You mean never? Why not?
ABRAHAM. *(Shrugs.)* Money.
MARY. Money?
ABRAHAM. To pay for you. Didn't you wonder where I got it?
MARY. Sometimes.
ABRAHAM. I steal it. From churches, who let me in to pray. From fools, who trust holy men. An Abbot found me out. He won't condemn me, if we stop now.
MARY. And if we don't?
ABRAHAM. I leave the Church. Take you, and go live — in the world.
MARY. Oh.
ABRAHAM. Man and wife, like other people. *(Mary sits up, frowning.)* Would you like that?
MARY. I'm not sure.
ABRAHAM. To tell you the truth, as much as I adore you, I rather like living around men. The discipline, the prayers. Marriage and babies and listening to women, I don't know.
MARY. Well, to tell you the truth, as much as I adore you, I like living with women. Marriage and babies and listening to *men*, I don't know.
ABRAHAM. I guess it's settled.
MARY. I guess it is.
ABRAHAM. We have to decide what to do with you.
MARY. Don't leave me here!
ABRAHAM. I thought you liked it here.
MARY. They'd put me in the bull pen.
ABRAHAM. Bull pen?
MARY. Men standing in line. Ten, sometimes twenty an hour!
ABRAHAM. Where do you want to go then?

HROSVITHA. There is only one place.
MARY. Where women are. If not a whorehouse, a convent.
HROSVITHA. Of course.
MARY. Can you arrange it?
HROSVITHA. I can.
MARY. Thank you, Abraham.
ABRAHAM. You're welcome, Mary. *(They look fondly at each other.)* I will miss you.
MARY. I will miss you, too. *(Abraham reaches out to her.)*
ABRAHAM. I will pray for you. *(Mary takes his hand.)*
MARY. And I will pray for you. *(Hrosvitha moves between them, a hand on each shoulder.)*
HROSVITHA. *(Fondly. To Mary.)* You will live with women. *(To Abraham.)* You will become an Abbot. And I? I will write more plays. *(Blackout.)*

AKHMATOVA

*from the poetry of Anna Akhmatova
and Osip Mandelstam*

for Kathleen Chalfant

CHARACTERS

PECDOV
MARYA
RUDINSKY
KLARINA
ANNA AKHMATOVA

PLACE

Moscow.

TIME

10 a.m. March 6, 1953.

AKHMATOVA

A red flag against a black wall.

An elegant carpet. A sturdy table with two chairs on each side. On the table is a cigarette box and ashtray, matches. Two other chairs downstage on each side.

Morning light. A deep bell tolls.

Pecdov stands in the light, at ease, relentlessly cheerful. Marya sits. She is terrified, trying not to show it.

PECDOV. Stalin, dead. Difficult to believe. Hard to grasp. *(He mimes closing a window. The bell is shut out. He turns to Marya.)* It is about ten pages long. Divided into many sections. A poem. We don't know the title.
MARYA. I see.
PECDOV. It is about a woman standing in front of a prison.
MARYA. I see.
PECDOV. She is waiting.
MARYA. I see.
PECDOV. *(Smiling.)* Please say something beside "I see." You sound pedantic.
MARYA. I'm sorry.
PECDOV. Such poems, given out in pieces for different people to memorize, exist like that. Unwritten. To be assembled. The existence of this one is alarming. Why? We'll see. *(Pause. He stares at her a moment, smiling.)* Well, old woman, standing in line. Thinking, probably, poetic thoughts. Anything wrong with that?
MARYA. If her thoughts are a danger to the state, yes.
PECDOV. How could they be? Some old bag of bones? But then, another woman becomes involved. She is also standing in the prison line. What does she say?
MARYA. How should I know?

PECDOV.   Guess.
MARYA.   How the old women could threaten the state?
PECDOV.   That's better.
MARYA.   They know something. State secrets?
PECDOV.   They have no knowledge of anything about the government. Try again.
MARYA.   One old woman is the poet?
PECDOV.   Brilliant.
MARYA.   And the other is like the reader. Audience. You and me.
PECDOV.   You are capable of marvels.
MARYA.   They have made someone in the government angry.
PECDOV.   Exasperated, better word. Would you like a cigarette?
MARYA.   No, thank you.
PECDOV.   Do you mind if I smoke?
MARYA.   Please do.
PECDOV.   Well, maybe I won't. *(He doesn't smoke.)* Try again. Personal life. Husband, say.
MARYA.   The poet is married to the wrong person.
PECDOV.   She was once but he died. You're getting close.
MARYA.   She is accusing someone of something.
PECDOV.   Stay where you were. Not marriage, but what comes next?
MARYA.   Children?
PECDOV.   Children. Exactly. This old woman, well, maybe not so old as I've made out, late forties, let's say, and in an oriental sort of way, quite handsome — she has a child. In the prison.
MARYA.   Oh. *(Pause.)* Akhmatova.
PECDOV.   Good for you. *(Smiling.)* Ever met her?
MARYA.   You know I have.
PECDOV.   I'm glad we're being straightforward with each other. One of the women in line: Anna Andreyevna Akhmatova. The other an old hag. Then, ten pages of poetry, saying we know not what, and at the very end, something overwhelming. Stupendous. But that's all we know. Ever meet Gumilev,

her son?
MARYA.   After he was in prison.
PECDOV.   The first time? That was in the thirties.
MARYA.   When I was a child.
PECDOV.   Set free to fight in the Army. War over, his grateful nation puts him in prison again. In and out and in, like that. I wonder why?
MARYA.   His mother.
PECDOV.   Um, and out of her son's tragedy she makes yet another poem, possibly treason. Poets are persistent, I'll say that for them. Now what? *(Pause.)* Do you like this room? It has always been used for these polite discussions. One of my predecessors, years ago, had Turgenev here. He was a young man then. So handsome, enormous shocks of hair. So rich. Mama's enormous hunks of the motherland. A thousand slaves. He had written a story. Do you know what he was told? Right here?
MARYA.   No.
PECDOV.   Given a brandy first. A Minister of Culture, no doubt quite like me, congratulated him. "Welcome, Ivan Sergeevich, to Russian letters!" "Thank you." There was a moment: Turgenev waiting to hear what was to be cut from his story, and the Minister like me waiting to strike to the heart of the matter. Which he did.
MARYA.   I see.
PECDOV.   *(Quickly.)* You *see?*
MARYA.   I beg your pardon! I don't see! What happened then?
PECDOV.   Turgenev finally blurted out, "Well, come now! What do you want cut?" Would you call that rude?
MARYA.   Uh, yes.
PECDOV.   I wouldn't. He asked an honest question. He got an honest answer. "We don't want to change a word of what you have written," said the man like me. "We just want to break its spirit." *(Pause.)* You *see?* *(Pause.)* Do you have any idea of what I'm saying?
MARYA.   Not quite, no.
PECDOV.   Well. We sit here in this same room, almost a century later, and I am saying the same thing, this time about

a woman who stood in a line in front of a prison and then didn't write down a poem about it. Whatever that is, I want to break its spirit, but I don't know what that spirit is, or what it says. I only know who possesses it.
MARYA. Akhmatova.
PECDOV. But why should I call you in, someone who knows her only slightly?
MARYA. You know I know her very well.
PECDOV. Yes, I do know that. But still, why? To ask you what she wrote?
MARYA. To ask if it threatens you.
PECDOV. Absolutely, and not just in the spirit. A real threat, in revolutionary terms. You love your country, don't you?
MARYA. Yes.
PECDOV. You wouldn't do anything to hurt her, would you?
MARYA. Never.
PECDOV. Do you think Akhmatova would?
MARYA. No, I don't.
PECDOV. How do you know?
MARYA. Her patriotic poems mean what they say. She wrote poems in praise of Stalin, too.
PECDOV. I know she wrote them and I know why and it wasn't for the love of Comrade Stalin. It was to keep her son from being executed. At the end of this poem, there is something else. What? Don't know. But whatever it is, people weep at the thought of it. So moved, they give Akhmatova money. Food. They help her live. What is it?
MARYA. I don't know. *(Pause.)*
PECDOV. In her early poems there are always lovers. Lovers, lovers. Zhdanov called her half nun, half whore. Do you know many writers like that?
MARYA. I know many writers who would like to be like that.
PECDOV. Artistic wit is so delicious when a country needs patriots. *(Pause.)* Anna Akhmatova is a relic of the Russian past. Living on, because of a talent, gift, yes, remarkable, for writing artistic ditties. Impressive as verse, perhaps: accurate, specific, surprising, melodious in her blunt way, sticking in the mind. But what is it about? Personal superiority, that's

what it's about!! Nostalgia for a childhood in the city of the Tsars, and how beautiful were the pine trees! Young lieutenants committing suicide! Great artists, mysterious doubles! All this bunk steaming in the rotten fumes of sick Christian mysticism, and the stink of Great Art. What could be worse for a Working People than a self-absorbed Nun/Whore Artiste! Our Soviet children, studying *her* in school? Today? Unthinkable! Stalin would get right out of his coffin. *(Smile.)* But I am always ready to learn. *(Pause.)* Who is the other woman in her poem?
MARYA.   I don't know.
PECDOV.   I have asked you two questions. What revelation is at the end of the poem and who is the old woman at the beginning. You say you don't know. Can you anticipate the next question?
MARYA.   No.
PECDOV.   Simple. Have you read the poem? But, wait, I haven't asked you yet. I don't want to, because then if you say you haven't, we face real difficulties. I haven't asked you anything yet. Nothing can be done to you yet. All right?
MARYA.   Yes.
PECDOV.   You're shaking. You've said nothing wrong. You are a valued worker, a teacher, respected by your students. However, once I ask you that question, then — we're in the soup. Your job, husband, children and so on. Do I have to ask? *(Long pause.)*
MARYA.   She gave me five words to remember. And I know the title. Requiem.
PECDOV.   Requiem? *(Laughs.)* Not for Stalin, that's certain. For her son? Maybe. For our government? Maybe. Only five words?
MARYA.   That's all.
PECDOV.   Do you expect me to believe that?
MARYA.   It's the truth!
PECDOV.   Why only five words?
MARYA.   I don't know. Maybe she didn't trust me.
PECDOV.   What are the five words?
MARYA.   River. Cows. Doves. Rain. Statue.

PECDOV. What?
MARYA. Key words, maybe. I think for the ending of the poem, but she didn't say that.
PECDOV. This is all you have to tell me?
MARYA. It's all I know.
PECDOV. Statue. Whose?
MARYA. I don't know that, either.
PECDOV. Statue, statue. There is no statue in front of that prison.
MARYA. I didn't think so.
PECDOV. What else? What *else?*
MARYA. Anna Andreyevna told me nothing else. I swear it.
PECDOV. *(Smiling.)* I see. Wait outside, with the others.
MARYA. You're smiling.
PECDOV. I begin my day with joy, and end it with joy. In between, I smile a lot. Wait outside. *(Exit Marya, as fast as she can.)* Hm. *(Blackout. Lights up on Pecdov with Rudinsky, a man in shabby, worn clothes.)* You'll have to do better than that!
RUDINSKY. He just won't talk about his mother.
PECDOV. But does he know about it?
RUDINSKY. You mean her poem?
PECDOV. No, *the end of the world.* Sit down!
RUDINSKY. You mean her poem?
PECDOV. *(Sighs.)* God damn it.
RUDINSKY. Forgive me, but I have been given very peculiar instructions! Go to prison! Get to know a man! Find out about his mother! I am performing this duty to the very best of my ability but I can't threaten him! I can't work him over! I can't get *at* him! God damn it yourself! I beg your pardon.
PECDOV. Frustrated, are you? Have to know why you are doing what you are doing? *(Pause.)* All right. Stalin died Sunday, after an all night dinner with Beria, Bulganin, Khrushchev, and Malenkov. A purge was on. At the top. At the *very* top. Put it together. Well? *Well?*
RUDINSKY. *(Aghast.)* They murdered Stalin?
PECDOV. It's possible. Cerebral hemorrhages can be brought

about. Now, a rising Minister of Culture, in my position, does what?
RUDINSKY.   Something threatening none of them.
PECDOV.   Of course, but what?
RUDINSKY.   Nothing?
PECDOV.   Fatal. It would be like I was waiting.
RUDINSKY.   Some — ah — useful activity? Involving some general security? Like that?
PECDOV.   Maybe. One of them will take over, but who? Everything is in the whirlwind. Anything can happen. Even a revolution, a real one this time. Zhdanov always said Anna Akhmatova was a traitor. Now she is writing an invisible poem about prisons and old women with endings that make people weep. What could it mean?
RUDINSKY.   My God, another revolution?
PECDOV.   Maybe. Maybe. Does the son know about her poems?
RUDINSKY.   He knows she writes about him. But he doesn't know what.
PECDOV.   Does he still hate his mother?
RUDINSKY.   Well, some. She farmed him out to his grandmother. She was a poet instead of a mother. He remembers her with bitterness. I did get that out of him.
PECDOV.   Did you tell him Stalin is dead?
RUDINSKY.   Yesterday. He won't talk to me at all now.
PECDOV.   Did he believe something would happen upon the death of Stalin?
RUDINSKY.   I think so.
PECDOV.   Did he say anything about any specific poem? With something overwhelming at the end of it?
RUDINSKY.   No. *(Long pause.)*
PECDOV.   Ah! Damn!
RUDINSKY.   I did the best I could. With my hands tied behind my back!
PECDOV.   I know that. Wait outside. *(Pecdov shakes hands with Rudinsky, claps him on the back. Exit Rudinsky. Blackout. Light on Pedcov and Klarina, a well dressed woman in her forties. She is fierce and intelligent. She suffers from many psychological wounds.)* And the

title of it, evidently, is "Requiem." What I need to find out is what happens at the end of it.
KLARINA. *(Paces.)* And you think *I* can find out?
PECDOV. You of all people. Do you understand why?
KLARINA. Because she loved me, and doesn't know what I did to her.
PECDOV. *(Smiles.)* Yes. Anna Andreyevna was so popular. The plainest people loved her steamy little verses, and I'll admit it, her. Stalin is dead. I want you to put those two things together? Can you?
KLARINA. No.
PECDOV. My dear woman, our great, vast, enormous land, our Soviet Russia, never had a revolution. Not a real one. Powers shifted. The backbone similarities between our government and the Russia of the Tsars are too obvious to need comment. We changed, yes, but not like France, or America. The thought of a truly popular revolution in our colossal country is not to be endured. Those who might bring it about must be dealt with. Now Stalin is gone. The one man who made a real revolution unthinkable is dead. And it is thinkable now. *(He stares at her.)* Are you all right?
KLARINA. Yes. I have a headache.
PECDOV. Four popular artists. Friends. Mandelstam, Marina Tsvetaeva, Pasternak, Akhmatova. Only she survived. Why?
KLARINA. She is a great poet.
PECDOV. Of a sort, maybe.
KLARINA. People *love* the poems. Half Russia recites Akhmatova.
PECDOV. Good. Defend her.
KLARINA. She refused to emigrate. She wrote passionately about staying with her country. She wrote a war poem praising Stalin.
PECDOV. All right. Mandelstam, labor camp. Tsvetaeva, suicide. Pasternak, muzzled. But Akhmatova remains, cooking up some deadly invisible opus called Requiem, of *what*, we may well ask! Do you follow me?
KLARINA. A revolution *after* Stalin? That's very doubtful. We loved Stalin. Didn't we?

PECDOV. *(Quickly.)* Of course we did! But a group begins now. Establishes something. Keeps on. In a year, five? I want you to talk to her again.
KLARINA. *(Paces.)* You can't ask me to do that.
PECDOV. Why not?
KLARINA. When she stood outside the prison walls, in those awful lines, she had time to think. She knows it was somebody's idea.
PECDOV. Which worked very well.
KLARINA. Do you know why I did that to her?
PECDOV. You love your country.
KLARINA. Yes, but something else.
PECDOV. She took a man away from you?
KLARINA. She is Dante!
PECDOV. And you are a Russian patriot. That's better than being Dante. You will try again. Right now.
KLARINA. She's *here?*
PECDOV. In the next room. Waiting, she thinks, to see her son.
KLARINA. Oh my God.
PECDOV. When she comes in, she will find you here instead. Her friend who put her son away in the first place. Elegant.
KLARINA. What do you have to know?
PECDOV. The old woman. That ending. Listen. Troops surround Moscow this instant. Tanks at every crossroad. This city is sealed off, but by an army ready to do God knows what under orders from God knows who!
KLARINA. Remember, she had a husband shot! She has a son in chains!
PECDOV. Oh yes, I know that. If Russia faces chaos, who cares? Here, smoke. If you get nowhere, don't worry. I'll be listening. *(Exit Pecdov. Blackout. Lights up on Anna Akhmatova. She has just entered the room. She is staring, stricken, at Klarina. She sinks into a chair. She is a middle aged woman, once a slim, imperious beauty, now growing pleasantly fat. She is a little unkempt, but erect, and self possessed. For many, she is the greatest poet in Russia.)*
ANNA. Oh. *(She sits in the chair, devastated. Klarina moves to the other chair, sits by her.)*

KLARINA. This is cruel.
ANNA. Yes.
KLARINA. I didn't send for you.
ANNA. I believe you.
KLARINA. I don't know where your son is, or what is happening to him. Have you heard anything?
ANNA. Not in three years.
KLARINA. You're looking very —
ANNA. Thanks to you! *(Pause.)*
KLARINA. Anna! *(Pause.)* You've known, all this time? *(Anna nods.)*
KLARINA. It wasn't just me, you know! It was the obvious thing to do to you. Stalin had so much trouble with his own son, when it was suggested to him, he said it was the perfect solution.
ANNA. He was right. You were right. It was. *(Pause.)*
KLARINA. Well. What are you writing now?
ANNA. Poetry in praise of Stalin.
KLARINA. I mean, anything else?
ANNA. Nothing else.
KLARINA. *(Paces.)* Just tell me, please? It's what they have to know! What else can I do but ask you, my darling?
ANNA. Nothing.
KLARINA. So tell me!
ANNA. Nothing. I've written nothing.
KLARINA. They know about Requiem.
ANNA. About what?
KLARINA. The old woman standing in line at the prisons. You are writing a poem about her, and it is considered possibly dangerous.
ANNA. An old woman in a prison line, dangerous?
KLARINA. If the old woman is created by Anna Akhmatova, yes!
ANNA. Interesting, as always, how your minds work.
KLARINA. It is your mind and how *it* works, Anna Andreyevna, they are worrying about!
ANNA. You are still beautiful.
KLARINA. What's in the poem?

ANNA. Men once wasted away for us.
KLARINA. What overwhelming thing happens at the end of that poem?
ANNA. We drove them crazy.
KLARINA. I am very sorry to tell you that I am not the only one of your friends from the past to betray you! Others have too!
ANNA. Most. The day Zhdanov attacked me, I hadn't read the papers. I slept in, went to market. I bought my fish, wrapped in a newspaper. I went home, unwrapped my fish. Newspaper, article, Zhdanov. Death to the poet. My son in prison again. I thought it was you.
KLARINA. God, my head! *(Enter Marya.)*
MARYA. Good afternoon.
KLARINA. You, too?
MARYA. Yes. You're getting nowhere. But stay. *(They sit in the chairs D., facing Anna.)*
MARYA. How are you, Anna Andreyevna?
ANNA. Well, thank you.
MARYA. I wish I was.
ANNA. So do I.
MARYA. Has Klarina told you what I've done?
KLARINA. No.
MARYA. I told them what I knew about Requiem.
ANNA. Oh.
MARYA. You can imagine why.
ANNA. Yes.
MARYA. It was a boy.
ANNA. So I heard.
MARYA. They can do to my son what they did to yours. Or worse.
ANNA. Yes.
MARYA. So I told them my five words.
ANNA. I see.
MARYA. They think it's the old way of passing poetry on, but different, somehow, and worse.
ANNA. I see.
KLARINA. They think it is dangerous.

MARYA. They're afraid you are writing about something to come after the death of Stalin.
KLARINA. What happens at the end of Requiem, Anna? That's what they have to know!
MARYA. They'll take it out of you, when they want to!
KLARINA. They believe us when we say we don't know what happens!
MARYA. But that can change!
KLARINA. You know we *don't* know!
MARYA. We could die!
KLARINA. If they don't find out!
MARYA. It's only a poem!
KLARINA. They can shoot us all!
MARYA. Your son! Mine!
KLARINA. You have to tell us, Anna!
MARYA. You have to tell us something! *(Pause.)*
ANNA. I will tell you this. If you love Russia, you can dig for her.
MARYA. What?
KLARINA. Dig? For something buried?
KLARINA and MARYA. Where?
ANNA. In Petersburg. Where Mandelstam said it was.
KLARINA. Mandelstam?
MARYA. Petersburg?
ANNA. I'm tired now. We had many good times, the three of us. When you were little, Marya, and Klarina loved the voice of God. No more.
KLARINA. The voice of God?
ANNA. That's what poetry is. You've forgotten. Goodbye. *(She closes her eyes.)*
KLARINA. Anna.
MARYA. Anna.
KLARINA and MARYA. Anna! *(Pause. Anna seems to be asleep. Enter Rudinsky.)*
RUDINSKY. I'll wake her up. *(He slams a chair down directly in front of Anna, and sits in it.)* I have been living with your son. In the same cell. He isn't where you think he is. He is here. In Moscow. Maybe five blocks from here. Look at me!

(Anna keeps her eyes shut.) I can get to him in an hour. I can tell him things. Imagine. *(Rudinsky gets up, speaks directly into her ear.)* He is going free. He will rot in a camp til he dies. His mother has used him to write a poem, for which he can be shot! *(Anna opens her eyes.)*
ANNA.   Five blocks?
RUDINSKY.   Five blocks. *(Satisfied, he sits down again.)* You've been playing games with your son's life.
ANNA.   Games? Do you think, after all these years, waiting to see him again, I would refuse tell you anything on earth? You silenced me as no other human being who ever lived. Tell me I can see him, and I will tell you anything you ask me.
RUDINSKY.   What happens to the old woman? What happens at the end of the poem? *That's* what you can tell us!
ANNA.   All right, but do I see my son?
RUDINSKY.   I can't promise, but yes, probably!
MARYA.   Anna, you gave me rain, a cow, boats and a statue. Is it the statue? Of someone — revolutionary?
ANNA.   If I tell you, will that set him free?
RUDINSKY.   It might!
KLARINA.   Tell us, Anna!
MARYA.   Please, Anna! *(Enter Pecdov. He carries a decanter of brandy and two glasses.)*
PECDOV.   "We will meet in Petersburg, around the grave where we buried the sun." She'll tell me now. Out. *(Exeunt Marya, Klarina and Rudinsky. Pecdov takes the chair Rudinsky had set in front of Anna and puts it back in place. He pours a brandy and hands it to her.)* Brandy?
ANNA.   Thank you. *(Pecdov pours himself a brandy.)*
PECDOV.   To a statue buried in the tomb of the sun. To your good health.
ANNA.   To yours. *(They sip the brandy.)*
PECDOV.   So. Here we are.
ANNA.   You've done very well.
PECDOV.   Yes, I have. The faithful disciple. Who sat at the feet of the master poets, with such humility. Such devotion to the great causes, until I discovered the great causes were the great egos of the great poets. Skillful parasites, just like Plato

said, feeding on the state. So I became a Minister of the People, and slept well at night.
ANNA. I am glad you sleep well at night.
PECDOV. Let us go back to Petersburg. To the grave of the sun.
ANNA. All right.
PECDOV. I remember it, too. Better than you, perhaps. *(Pecdov closes his eyes and recites, broadly, in the Russian manner.)* "We will meet in Petersburg, around the grave where we buried the sun —" *(Anna closes her eyes, and recites.)*
ANNA. "And then together we will say it for the first time, the wonderful word meaning nothing —" *(Both, eyes closed, recite.)*
PECDOV. *(Reciting.)* "In the new Russian night, soft and beautiful darkness, a black velvet nowhere, the beloved eyes of sacred women are still singing, flowers blossom that will live forever —
ANNA. *(Reciting.)* "The city gathers itself like a lost cat, soldiers are stationed on the bridges, one automobile dashes blindly by, siren whooping like a screaming bird —
PECDOV. *(Reciting.)* "Tonight I will not carry my credentials, I have no fear of the soldiers. I will pray in the new Russian night, for the wonderful word meaning nothing —
ANNA. *(Reciting.)* "For fun we will stand by a fire, maybe time will fall apart, and the beloved hands of sacred women will sweep the ashes back together —
PECDOV. *(Reciting.)* "Don't worry when the candles all snuff out, in the soft and beautiful darkness, the black nowhere. The bent shoulders of sacred women are still singing —
PECDOV and ANNA. *(Reciting.)* "You will not see the sun, still burning in the night." *(Pause.)*
PECDOV. Mandelstam.
ANNA. Mandelstam.
PECDOV. And poetry, the voice of God. Do you know how he died?
ANNA. No.
PECDOV. Paranoid in a camp, certain his filthy grub was being poisoned. He tried to stay alive by stealing food from

other prisoners. They beat him to death. Great poet of the Russian land.
ANNA. I am not surprised.
PECDOV. I denounced him to Stalin.
ANNA. I am not surprised.
PECDOV. He read ten of us a poem about Stalin, in which Stalin had cockroach eyebrows, and greasy fingers staining pages of books by men he would kill. It was the single denunciation of Stalin ever written down by anyone, and that one poem did it. Now it is your turn. But you are different. Not as a poet. As a mother.
ANNA. How ingenious, the Devil. Killing a woman with her son. Mephistopheles, blush.
PECDOV. I always forget the Christian part of you. The nun within the whore. Never mind Mephistopheles. While Stalin lived, your son was safe. Kept in prison, used to torment you, but not to be killed. Now Stalin is gone, and others will make that decision. Who is the statue that makes people weep? *(Anna doesn't answer.)* I can let him go. You can be drinking champagne with him in half an hour. Or he can be shot. Not another second. Is there a statue?
ANNA. Yes. *(Pecdov gets up.)*
PECDOV. Of someone revolutionary?
ANNA. Yes.
PECDOV. Making Russia weep?
ANNA. Yes.
PECDOV. Who?
ANNA. I am the statue.
PECDOV. What?
ANNA. I stand in front of that prison. My metal eyes weep tears. In my poem, I am the statue.
PECDOV. I don't understand.
ANNA. Of course not.
PECDOV. You have built a statue to *yourself?*
ANNA. Yes. *(Pause. Pecdov laughs, richly and loudly, sits.)*
PECDOV. Made yourself a monument? Made yourself *an icon?*
ANNA. *(To him, explaining it.)* I have made a statue of an old woman, standing in a line outside a prison, waiting every day

to see her son. In the line are many other women, with sons, daughters, husbands, sisters, mothers and fathers. All in prison. And to my country I say, if in some future year, you mark my life with a statue, I consent to that honor. But I will not stand in the gardens of my love affairs, or in the company of the splendid artists I have known, or before the applauding crowds who loved me, but there, in a line of women, by the riverboats and the doves, before an iron gate, which was never, not once, opened to me. Russia can remember me there, if she pleases.
PECDOV.   My God! All this fuss! Anna Andreyevna, you are not a dangerous revolutionary. You are crazy old woman.
ANNA.   And you are an insect of a single day. *(A long pause.)*
PECDOV.   It's not his fault your son has a madwoman for a mother. If I make an issue of this, I'll put myself up for ridicule. Keep your mouth shut and go in peace.
ANNA.   Will I ever see him again?
PECDOV.   Soon, maybe. Stalin is dead, who knows what will happen. Never, maybe. Stalin is dead, who knows what will happen. Goodbye. *(Anna nods and starts to exit.)* Certainly — *(Anna stops.)* Statues will be made. But not of you. Of Stalin, and in time, perhaps, of me. *(Anna goes to him. He looks at her.)*
ANNA.   Perhaps. *(Exit Anna. Pecdov stands thinking. He opens the window again. The bell tolls for Stalin. Light fades on Pecdov, thinking.)*

PROPERTY LIST

KOMACHI
Samurai sword and scabbard

HROSVITHA
Handmade cross (Abraham)

AKHMATOVA
Decanter of brandy (Pecdov)
Two glasses (Pecdov)

COSTUME PLOT

KOMACHI
Noh mask, black kimono, white scarf (Komachi)
Colored trousers, no shirt, red scarf, sandals (Shosho)
Black sweater, trousers or skirt (Komachi's Voice)

HROSVITHA
Nun's habit (10th century German) (Hrosvitha)
Same as Hrosvitha, but with regal red trimming (Gerberga)
Hermit's robe, cloak, sandals, large, wide-brimmed hat
   (Abraham)
Simple white dress, a colorful, sexy shawl (Mary)
Monk's robe with hood, sandals (Brother William)

AKHMATOVA
Simple sweater and skirt, raincoat (carried) (Akhmatova)
Black suit and tie (Pecdov)
Worn and shabby suit and hat (Rudinsky)
Plain Russian woman's clothes (Marya)
Expensive woman's clothes, in good taste (Klarina)

SEASHORE TREE STUMP

SEASHORE ROCKS

"THREE POETS"
KOMACHI

(Designed by Anne C. Patterson for the Theater for the New City production.)

GOTHIC CHAIR

CARPET

GOTHIC CHAIR

"THREE POETS"
HROSVITHA

(Designed by Anne C. Patterson for the Theater for the New City production.)

"THREE POETS"
AKHMATOVA

(Designed by Anne C. Patterson for the Theater for the New City production.)

NEW PLAYS

★ **INTIMATE APPAREL by Lynn Nottage.** The moving and lyrical story of a turn-of-the-century black seamstress whose gifted hands and sewing machine are the tools she uses to fashion her dreams from the whole cloth of her life's experiences. "...Nottage's play has a delicacy and eloquence that seem absolutely right for the time she is depicting..." –*NY Daily News*. "...thoughtful, affecting...The play offers poignant commentary on an era when the cut and color of one's dress—and of course, skin—determined whom one could and could not marry, sleep with, even talk to in public." –*Variety*. [2M, 4W] ISBN: 0-8222-2009-1

★ **BROOKLYN BOY by Donald Margulies.** A witty and insightful look at what happens to a writer when his novel hits the bestseller list. "The characters are beautifully drawn, the dialogue sparkles..." –*nytheatre.com*. "Few playwrights have the mastery to smartly investigate so much through a laugh-out-loud comedy that combines the vintage subject matter of successful writer-returning-to-ethnic-roots with the familiar mid-life crisis." –*Show Business Weekly*. [4M, 3W] ISBN: 0-8222-2074-1

★ **CROWNS by Regina Taylor.** Hats become a springboard for an exploration of black history and identity in this celebratory musical play. "Taylor pulls off a Hat Trick: She scores thrice, turning CROWNS into an artful amalgamation of oral history, fashion show, and musical theater..." –*TheatreMania.com*. "...wholly theatrical...Ms. Taylor has created a show that seems to arise out of spontaneous combustion, as if a bevy of department-store customers simultaneously decided to stage a revival meeting in the changing room." –*NY Times*. [1M, 6W (2 musicians)] ISBN: 0-8222-1963-8

★ **EXITS AND ENTRANCES by Athol Fugard.** The story of a relationship between a young playwright on the threshold of his career and an aging actor who has reached the end of his. "[Fugard] can say more with a single line than most playwrights convey in an entire script...Paraphrasing the title, it's safe to say this drama, making its memorable entrance into our consciousness, is unlikely to exit as long as a theater exists for exceptional work." –*Variety*. "A thought-provoking, elegant and engrossing new play..." –*Hollywood Reporter*. [2M] ISBN: 0-8222-2041-5

★ **BUG by Tracy Letts.** A thriller featuring a pair of star-crossed lovers in an Oklahoma City motel facing a bug invasion, paranoia, conspiracy theories and twisted psychological motives. "...obscenely exciting...top-flight craftsmanship. Buckle up and brace yourself..." –*NY Times*. "...[a] thoroughly outrageous and thoroughly entertaining play...the possibility of enemies, real and imagined, to squash has never been more theatrical." –*A.P.* [3M, 2W] ISBN: 0-8222-2016-4

★ **THOM PAIN (BASED ON NOTHING) by Will Eno.** An ordinary man muses on childhood, yearning, disappointment and loss, as he draws the audience into his last-ditch plea for empathy and enlightenment. "It's one of those treasured nights in the theater—treasured nights anywhere, for that matter—that can leave you both breathless with exhilaration and...in a puddle of tears." –*NY Times*. "Eno's words...are familiar, but proffered in a way that is constantly contradictory to our expectations. Beckett is certainly among his literary ancestors." –*nytheatre.com*. [1M] ISBN: 0-8222-2076-8

★ **THE LONG CHRISTMAS RIDE HOME by Paula Vogel.** Past, present and future collide on a snowy Christmas Eve for a troubled family of five. "...[a] lovely and hauntingly original family drama...a work that breathes so much life into the theater." –*Time Out*. "...[a] delicate visual feast..." –*NY Times*. "...brutal and lovely...the overall effect is magical." –*NY Newsday*. [3M, 3W] ISBN: 0-8222-2003-2

DRAMATISTS PLAY SERVICE, INC.
440 Park Avenue South, New York, NY 10016 212-683-8960 Fax 212-213-1539
postmaster@dramatists.com   www.dramatists.com